Mathematics

Multiplication and Division

This book belongs to

_____

Welcome to Learning Express!

Helping your child build essential skills is easy!

These teacher-approved activities have been specially developed to make learning both accessible and enjoyable. On each page, you'll find:

Focus Skill
The focus of each activity page is clearly indicated.

Meaningful learning
Each activity has been carefully designed to make your child's learning meaningful and fun.

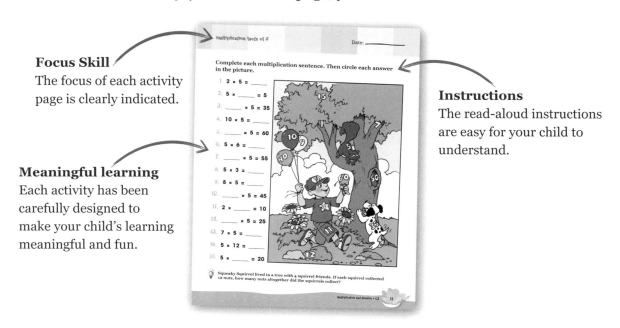

Instructions
The read-aloud instructions are easy for your child to understand.

This book also contains:

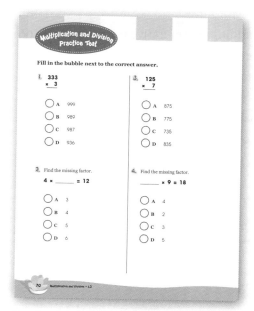

Instant assessment to ensure your child really masters the skills.

Completion certificate to celebrate your child's leap in learning.

Motivational stickers to mark the milestones of your child's learning path.

Contents

Multiplication and Division

When you multiply, you add a number to itself a number of times. For example: $4 + 4 + 4 + 4 + 4 = 20$ or $4 \times 5 = 20$. Multiplying is a quick way to add things up.

When you divide, you group numbers into equal parts. In the example $10 \div 2 = 5$, you group 10 into 2 equal parts of 5. To check your answer, you do the opposite of division — you multiply $5 \times 2 = 10$.

Sometimes you can't group all the numbers into equal parts. In those cases you will have a remainder, a number left over. For example: $38 \div 6 = 6$, remainder 2.

What to do

Have your child solve the multiplication and division problems on the activity pages. Review the answers with your child. Remind your child that he or she can check the division problems by multiplying. In the example $38 \div 6 = 6$ remainder 2, multiply $6 \times 6 + 2 = 38$. Your answer is correct! An answer key is provided at the back of the book for your convenience.

Keep On Going!

Show your child that math can be fun by playing a multiplication/division game together. Give your child a multiplication problem and have him or her solve it and then turn it into a division problem to check the answer.
For example:

$$7 \times 4 = 28$$
$$28 \div 4 = 7 \qquad \text{or} \qquad 28 \div 7 = 4$$

Date: _____

A **number line** can be used to help you multiply. One factor tells you how long each jump should be. This is like skip-counting the other factor tells you how many jumps to take.

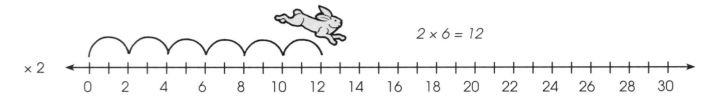

$2 \times 6 = 12$

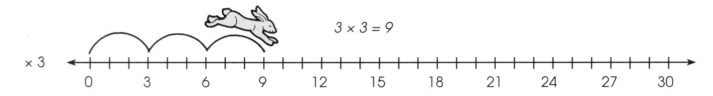

$3 \times 3 = 9$

Use the number lines above to help you multiply by 2s and 3s.

1. $2 \times 2 = $ _____ $3 \times 3 = $ _____ $6 \times 2 = $ _____

2. $4 \times 3 = $ _____ $9 \times 2 = $ _____ $7 \times 3 = $ _____

3. $7 \times 2 = $ _____ $6 \times 3 = $ _____ $5 \times 2 = $ _____

When multiplying by 0, the product is always 0. When multiplying by 1, the product is always the other factor.

4.
$$\begin{array}{r} 1 \\ \times\, 2 \\ \hline \end{array} \qquad \begin{array}{r} 8 \\ \times\, 3 \\ \hline \end{array} \qquad \begin{array}{r} 2 \\ \times\, 5 \\ \hline \end{array} \qquad \begin{array}{r} 0 \\ \times\, 3 \\ \hline \end{array} \qquad \begin{array}{r} 3 \\ \times\, 2 \\ \hline \end{array} \qquad \begin{array}{r} 2 \\ \times\, 7 \\ \hline \end{array}$$

5.
$$\begin{array}{r} 4 \\ \times\, 2 \\ \hline \end{array} \qquad \begin{array}{r} 3 \\ \times\, 3 \\ \hline \end{array} \qquad \begin{array}{r} 1 \\ \times\, 3 \\ \hline \end{array} \qquad \begin{array}{r} 6 \\ \times\, 2 \\ \hline \end{array} \qquad \begin{array}{r} 0 \\ \times\, 2 \\ \hline \end{array} \qquad \begin{array}{r} 3 \\ \times\, 1 \\ \hline \end{array}$$

Multiplication *is repeated addition using equal groups. The numbers being multiplied together are called* **factors**. *The answer is called the* **product**.

Read the problem and draw a model to show your answer.

> ### Example
>
> Charlie's coach bought 3 bags of hockey pucks. There are 4 pucks in each bag. How many pucks did he buy altogether?
>
> This problem can be solved by drawing a model.
>
> ⊙⊙ + ⊙⊙ + ⊙⊙ = 12 pucks
> ⊙⊙   ⊙⊙   ⊙⊙
>
>   3   ×   4   =   12 pucks
> factor   factor   product
>
> There are 3 equal groups of 4 pucks.

1. Charlie's team played 3 games. They scored 3 points in each game. How many points did they score in all? (Draw a box for each point.)

2. Charlie and his friend each have 4 hockey sticks. How many sticks do they have?

 On another sheet of paper, write your own word problem that involves repeated addition using equal groups. Ask a friend to solve it by drawing a model.

Date: _____

An **array** shows a multiplication sentence. The first factor tells how many rows there are. The second factor tells how many are in each row. Here is an array for the multiplication sentence $4 \times 4 = 16$.

$$\begin{array}{r} 4\,rows \\ \times \quad 4\,rows \\ \hline 16\,in\,all \end{array}$$

Solve each problem by creating an array.

1. **3 × 4 =**

2. **6 × 5 =**

3. **2 × 5 =**

4. **6 × 4 =**

5. **8 × 4 =**

6. **3 × 5 =**

Date: _____

A multiplication sentence can be diagrammed on a **coordinate grid**. To show 5×4, use the factors as the ordered pair $(5, 4)$. Then go over 5 and up 4 on the grid, and mark the point where the lines intersect to make a rectangle. Finally, count all the squares in the rectangle.

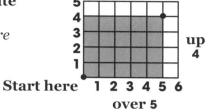

First, write the ordered pair for each set of multiplication factors. Then mark the intersecting point for the ordered pair on the grid. Color and count each square in the rectangle. Fill in the blank with the total number of squares that are in the rectangle.

1.

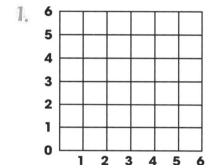

3 × 4 = (_____)

Total squares = ☐

2.

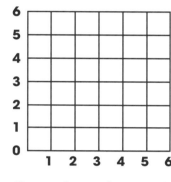

2 × 4 = (_____)

Total squares = ☐

3.

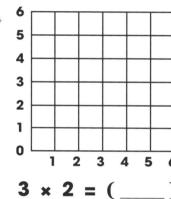

3 × 2 = (_____)

Total squares = ☐

4.

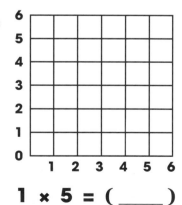

1 × 5 = (_____)

Total squares = ☐

5.

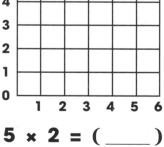

5 × 2 = (_____)

Total squares = ☐

6.

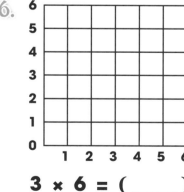

3 × 6 = (_____)

Total squares = ☐

Date: _____

Multiply. Write the number word for each product in the puzzle. Don't forget the hyphens!

Across

2. 4 × 9 = _____

4. 4 × 5 = _____

7. 4 × 3 = _____

8. 4 × 7 = _____

9. 4 × 10 = _____

11. 4 × 0 = _____

12. 4 × 11 = _____

Down

1. 4 × 4 = _____

2. 4 × 8 = _____

3. 4 × 12 = _____

5. 4 × 2 = _____

6. 4 × 6 = _____

10. 4 × 1 = _____

Tracy was missing 4 buttons on 11 different shirts. How many buttons does she need to fix all the shirts?

Complete each multiplication sentence. Then circle each answer in the picture.

1. 2 × 5 = _____

2. 5 × _____ = 5

3. _____ × 5 = 35

4. 10 × 5 = _____

5. _____ × 5 = 60

6. 5 × 6 = _____

7. _____ × 5 = 55

8. 5 × 3 = _____

9. 8 × 5 = _____

10. _____ × 5 = 45

11. 2 × _____ = 10

12. _____ × 5 = 25

13. 7 × 5 = _____

14. 5 × 12 = _____

15. 5 × _____ = 20

 Squeaky Squirrel lived in a tree with 4 squirrel friends. If each squirrel collected 12 nuts, how many nuts altogether did the squirrels collect?

Date: _____

Multiply. Then write the letter of the problem that matches each product below to learn the names of two of the brightest stars.

B   3
    × 4

R   1
    × 4

A   2
    × 4

F   8
    × 4

P   7
    × 4

S   6
    × 5

U   3
    × 5

E   1
    × 5

U   4
    × 4

I   5
    × 5

G   0
    × 5

S   2
    × 5

O   4 × 5 = ____

D   9 × 5 = ____

I   9 × 4 = ____

N   6 × 4 = ____

S   7 × 5 = ____

C   5 × 8 = ____

Two of the brightest stars are

___ ___ ___ ___ ___ ___   and   ___ ___ ___ ___ ___ ___ ___ .
10   25   4   36   16   30   49   8   24   20   28   15   35

Date: _____

**Multiply each number in the center by the numbers on the tire.
Write your answers inside the wheel.**

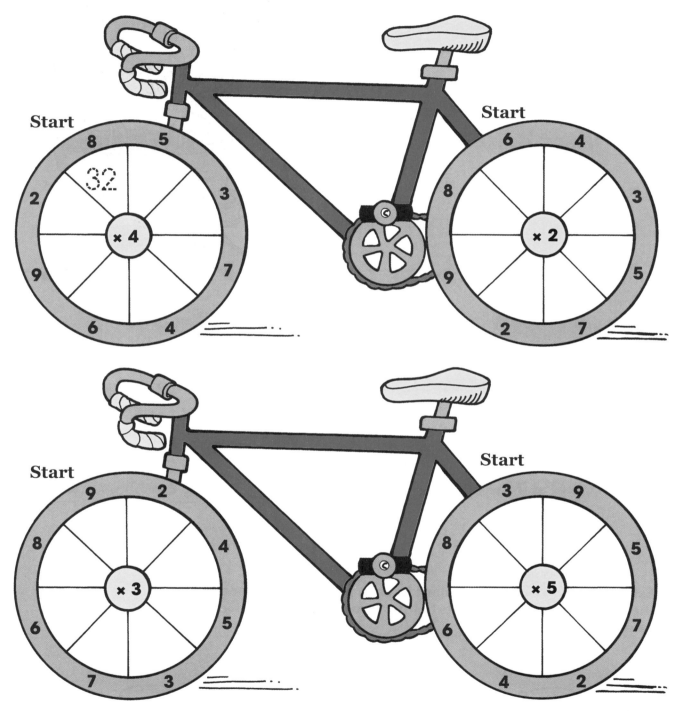

 The bike team has 4 members. Each biker rides 9 km every day. How many km does
the team ride every day altogether?

Date: _____

Multiply.

1. $6 \times 6 =$ _____ $2 \times 7 =$ _____

2. $1 \times 7 =$ _____ $5 \times 6 =$ _____

3. $2 \times 6 =$ _____ $4 \times 7 =$ _____

4. $0 \times 7 =$ _____ $7 \times 7 =$ _____

5.
$$\begin{array}{r} 6 \\ \times 7 \\ \hline \end{array} \qquad \begin{array}{r} 2 \\ \times 6 \\ \hline \end{array} \qquad \begin{array}{r} 9 \\ \times 7 \\ \hline \end{array} \qquad \begin{array}{r} 4 \\ \times 6 \\ \hline \end{array} \qquad \begin{array}{r} 6 \\ \times 6 \\ \hline \end{array} \qquad \begin{array}{r} 3 \\ \times 7 \\ \hline \end{array}$$

6.
$$\begin{array}{r} 3 \\ \times 6 \\ \hline \end{array} \qquad \begin{array}{r} 8 \\ \times 7 \\ \hline \end{array} \qquad \begin{array}{r} 1 \\ \times 6 \\ \hline \end{array} \qquad \begin{array}{r} 5 \\ \times 7 \\ \hline \end{array} \qquad \begin{array}{r} 9 \\ \times 6 \\ \hline \end{array} \qquad \begin{array}{r} 7 \\ \times 6 \\ \hline \end{array}$$

 Ashley bought 4 flowers to plant in each pot. She has 7 pots. How many flowers did she buy in all? Using the pots below, draw a model to solve the problem. Then write a number sentence.

Date: _____

Multiply. Write the number word for each product in the puzzle. Don't forget the hyphens!

Across

1. $9 \times 5 =$ ___   10. $9 \times 10 =$ ___

5. $1 \times 9 =$ ___   12. $2 \times 9 =$ ___

7. $9 \times 12 =$ ___   13. $9 \times 11 =$ ___

9. $4 \times 9 =$ ___

Down

2. $9 \times 3 =$ ___   6. $9 \times 8 =$ ___

3. $6 \times 9 =$ ___   8. $7 \times 9 =$ ___

4. $0 \times 9 =$ ___   11. $9 \times 9 =$ ___

Date: _____

Multiply to get the lion back to its little cub.

9 × 8 = _____

8 × 5 = _____

9
× 2

9 × 4 = _____

3 × 8 = _____

6
× 8

8 × 1 = _____

9 × 9 = _____

8 × 4 = _____

8
× 7

6 × 9 = _____

9 × 3 = _____

8 × 8 = _____

8
× 2

9 × 0 = _____

5 × 9 = _____

 There are 8 lions in the jungle. Each has 2 cubs. How many cubs are there altogether?

Date: _____

Multiply.

1.
$$9 \times 6$$ $$8 \times 9$$ $$8 \times 5$$ $$8 \times 6$$ $$8 \times 3$$

2.
$$9 \times 3$$ $$9 \times 9$$ $$7 \times 8$$ $$2 \times 9$$ $$4 \times 8$$

3.
$$9 \times 8$$ $$9 \times 0$$ $$2 \times 8$$ $$8 \times 8$$ $$6 \times 9$$

4.
$$9 \times 4$$ $$9 \times 7$$ $$1 \times 9$$ $$8 \times 4$$ $$0 \times 8$$

5.
$$3 \times 9$$ $$5 \times 8$$ $$7 \times 9$$ $$1 \times 8$$ $$5 \times 9$$

Circle the problem in Row 5 with the same product as 2 × 4.
Circle the problem in Row 4 with the same product as 3 × 3.
Circle the problem in Row 3 with the same product as 4 × 4.
Circle the problem in Row 2 with the same product as 6 × 3.
Circle the problem in Row 1 with the same product as 4 × 6.
Did you find your way to the top?

Date: _____

Complete the multiplication chart.

×	0	1	2	3	4	5	6	7	8	9
0				0						
1										
2		2								
3										
4										
5										
6										
7								49		
8										
9										

Using the chart, help Detective Dan find each missing factor.

1. $4 \times$ _____ $= 12$ $7 \times$ _____ $= 14$ $3 \times$ _____ $= 27$

2. $5 \times$ _____ $= 30$ $6 \times$ _____ $= 36$ $8 \times$ _____ $= 64$

3. _____ $\times 4 = 36$ _____ $\times 3 = 24$ _____ $\times 9 = 18$

4. _____ $\times 8 = 56$ _____ $\times 9 = 81$ _____ $\times 1 = 6$

 On another sheet of paper, write five missing factor number sentences. Have a friend solve them. Check your friend's work.

Date: _____

Multiply. Color each triangle with an even product orange. Color each triangle with an odd product blue.

8 × 6 = ___	9 × 4 = ___	8 × 9 = ___	8 × 2 = ___
7 × 9 = ___	7 × 7 = ___	9 × 3 = ___	3 × 5 = ___
7 × 7 = ___	4 × 6 = ___	8 × 7 = ___	1 × 7 = ___
8 × 8 = ___	9 × 5 = ___	5 × 7 = ___	8 × 10 = ___
6 × 9 = ___	9 × 9 = ___	7 × 3 = ___	6 × 6 = ___
5 × 5 = ___	5 × 8 = ___	6 × 3 = ___	9 × 7 = ___
1 × 9 = ___	5 × 9 = ___	7 × 5 = ___	3 × 9 = ___
7 × 10 = ___	7 × 6 = ___	9 × 8 = ___	6 × 10 = ___

Maria was decorating a picture frame for her friend's birthday. She chose seven different-sized, diamond-shaped tiles to glue around the frame. There was enough room to glue four colors of each size of tile. How many tiles did she use altogether to decorate the frame? On another sheet of paper, solve this problem and draw a picture of what the frame might look like.

Date: _____

 When multiplying the factor 11 by a number from 1 to 9, double the number to find the product.

Examples: $11 \times 5 = 55$ $11 \times 7 = 77$

Look at each multiplication sentence. If the product is correct, circle it. If the product is incorrect, cross it out and write the correct product above it.

$8 \times 11 = 81$ $3 \times 11 = 33$

$4 \times 11 = 48$

$5 \times 11 = 66$

$9 \times 11 = 99$

$11 \times 6 = 66$ $2 \times 11 = 22$

$7 \times 11 = 74$

$1 \times 11 = 12$

$6 \times 11 = 54$

$11 \times 2 = 21$

$11 \times 3 = 23$ $11 \times 8 = 88$

$11 \times 5 = 55$

FINE DINING

$11 \times 7 = 77$

$11 \times 4 = 44$ $11 \times 9 = 88$ $11 \times 1 = 11$

Date: _____

The rest of the multiplication facts with a factor of 11 are: 11 × 0 = 0, 11 × 10 = 110, 11 × 11 = 121, and 11 × 12 = 132. Since you cannot just double the number being multiplied by 11, these are the "tuffys."

Multiply. If the multiplication sentence is a "tuffy," color the space blue. If it is a double, color the space yellow.

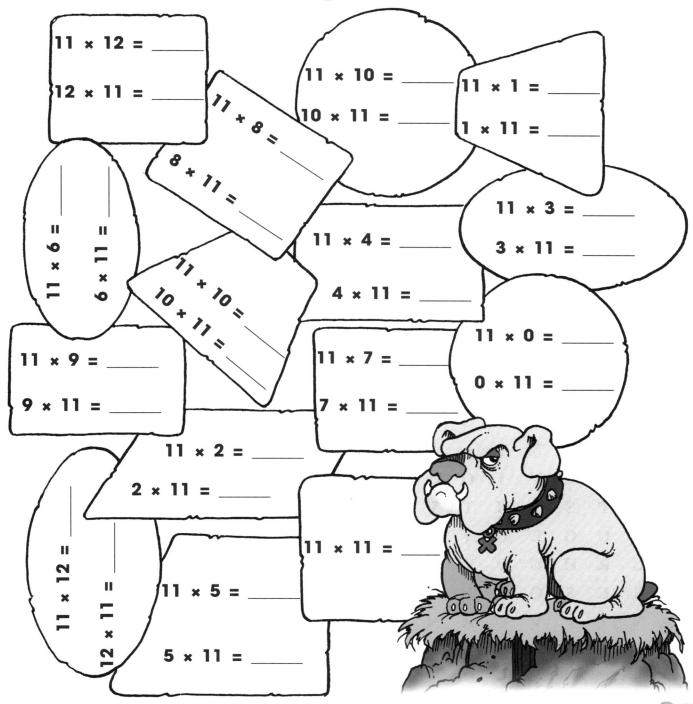

11 × 12 = _____

12 × 11 = _____

11 × 8 = _____

8 × 11 = _____

11 × 10 = _____

10 × 11 = _____

11 × 1 = _____

1 × 11 = _____

11 × 6 = _____

6 × 11 = _____

11 × 3 = _____

3 × 11 = _____

11 × 4 = _____

4 × 11 = _____

11 × 10 = _____

10 × 11 = _____

11 × 9 = _____

9 × 11 = _____

11 × 7 = _____

7 × 11 = _____

11 × 0 = _____

0 × 11 = _____

11 × 2 = _____

2 × 11 = _____

11 × 12 = _____

12 × 11 = _____

11 × 11 = _____

11 × 5 = _____

5 × 11 = _____

Date: _____

Multiply. Then circle the number word for each product in the puzzle. The words will go across, down and diagonally.

1. 12 × 0 = _____   12 × 4 = _____   12 × 7 = _____   12 × 10 = _____

2. 12 × 1 = _____   12 × 5 = _____   12 × 8 = _____   12 × 11 = _____

3. 12 × 2 = _____   12 × 6 = _____   12 × 9 = _____   12 × 12 = _____

4. 12 × 3 = _____

```
O N E H U N D R E D T H I R T Y – T W O
R N F X W F R Q R I P D B Q E H B H O P
E Q E Z T O O U C Z G S C I O D M I A F
O N E H U N D R E D E I G H T R T R T O
Y W I L U I G U N N R X D W L E N H Y R
M T E N V N H W T H I R T Y – S I X G T
E W F O N E D U K D L E A T R E B C Y Y
T E G N E T R R O H U T T D X E E O P –
Y N O H S Y H H E I G H T Y – F O U R E
P T I U E – G V B D H I D W N Q J N T I
L Y W N X S L I E E T R J F E I G H Y G
D – T H V I O W S N Y W J K F L B T N H
A F T S I X T Y O E T X E K O L V C K T
K O U G E U R E N I Y O N R Y V E T Z
T U R H U V D D Z S E V E N T Y – T W O
F R E S O N E F T E T Y F I X Y A Y E C
A N T F V U R N O R R M S O U T Y I R J
O N E H U N D R E D F O R T Y – F O U R
```

Date: _____

Write a multiplication fact on each blank using 12 as a factor for the product on each wastebasket. Use a different sentence for each product.

1.

 84
 0

_____   _____

2.

 96
 132
 72
 144
 36

_____   _____   _____   _____   _____

3.

 12
 60
 84
 108
 48

_____   _____   _____   _____   _____

4.

 120
 48
 96
 132
 24

_____   _____   _____   _____   _____

 Elizabeth wrote 12 different multiplication sentences on each of 6 different pieces of paper. After solving all the problems, she discovered 5 of the problems had the same product. On another piece of paper, show how many multiplication sentences Elizabeth wrote in all. Then write 5 multiplication sentences with the same product.

Date: _____

Use a stopwatch to time how long it takes to multiply around the obstacle course.

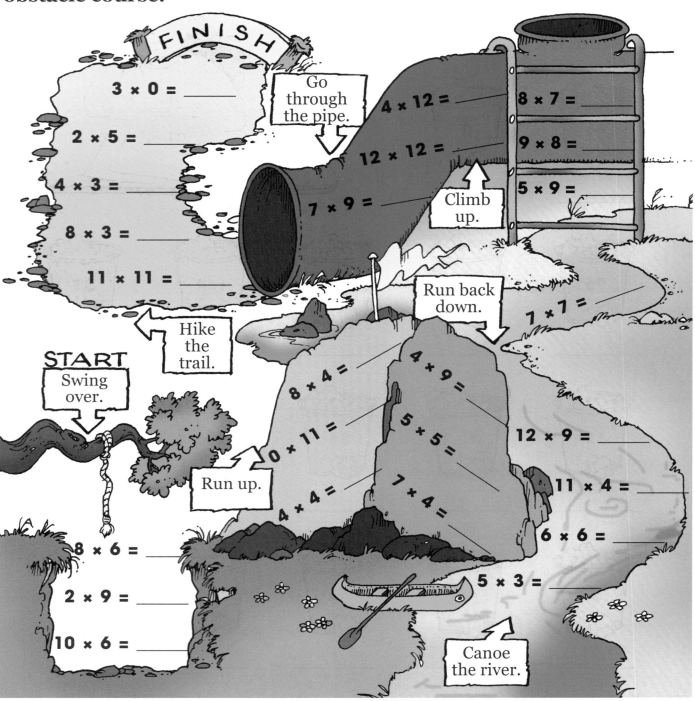

FINISH

3 × 0 = _____

2 × 5 = _____

4 × 3 = _____

8 × 3 = _____

11 × 11 = _____

Go through the pipe.

4 × 12 = _____

12 × 12 = _____

7 × 9 = _____

Climb up.

8 × 7 = _____

9 × 8 = _____

5 × 9 = _____

Hike the trail.

Run back down.

7 × 7 = _____

START

Swing over.

8 × 4 = _____

0 × 11 = _____

Run up.

4 × 4 = _____

4 × 9 = _____

5 × 5 = _____

7 × 4 = _____

12 × 9 = _____

11 × 4 = _____

6 × 6 = _____

8 × 6 = _____

2 × 9 = _____

10 × 6 = _____

5 × 3 = _____

Canoe the river.

 In the morning, four students completed the obstacle course. In the afternoon, five students completed the same course. If each student completed the course seven times, how many times altogether was the course completed?

Date: _____

Multiply. Then use the code to answer the riddle below.

A **10 × 10 =**   G **3 × 1 =**   N **12 × 8 =**   S **6 × 9 =**

B **6 × 7 =**   H **9 × 9 =**   O **6 × 6 =**   T **6 × 0 =**

C **5 × 6 =**   I **8 × 9 =**   P **11 × 12 =**   U **5 × 8 =**

E **7 × 7 =**   L **12 × 2 =**   Q **8 × 8 =**   V **7 × 3 =**

F **3 × 9 =**   M **3 × 6 =**   R **4 × 5 =**   Y **2 × 8 =**

Why are multiplicationists so successful?

$\overline{49}$ $\overline{21}$ $\overline{49}$ $\overline{20}$ $\overline{16}$ $\overline{132}$ $\overline{20}$ $\overline{36}$ $\overline{42}$ $\overline{24}$ $\overline{49}$ $\overline{18}$

$\overline{0}$ $\overline{81}$ $\overline{49}$ $\overline{16}$ $\overline{49}$ $\overline{96}$ $\overline{30}$ $\overline{36}$ $\overline{40}$ $\overline{96}$ $\overline{0}$ $\overline{49}$ $\overline{20}$

$\overline{72}$ $\overline{96}$ $\overline{24}$ $\overline{72}$ $\overline{27}$ $\overline{49}$

$\overline{42}$ $\overline{49}$ $\overline{30}$ $\overline{36}$ $\overline{18}$ $\overline{49}$ $\overline{54}$ $\overline{100}$

$\overline{30}$ $\overline{81}$ $\overline{100}$ $\overline{24}$ $\overline{24}$ $\overline{49}$ $\overline{96}$ $\overline{3}$ $\overline{49}$

$\overline{0}$ $\overline{36}$ $\overline{30}$ $\overline{36}$ $\overline{96}$ $\overline{64}$ $\overline{40}$ $\overline{49}$ $\overline{20}$!

Date: _____

Multiply around the bases. Start at first base on each baseball field. Then multiply the number on each base in order. Write each product on home plate.

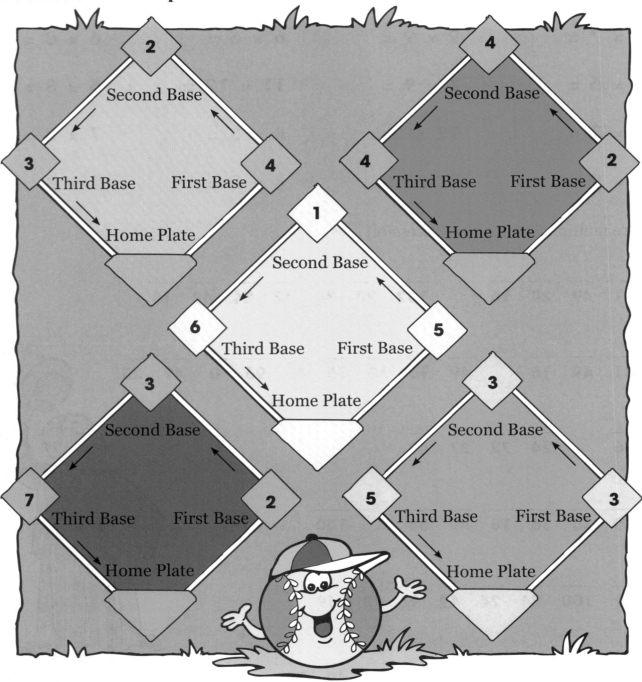

 Four players each have 2 boxes of balls. There are 4 balls in each box. How many balls do the players have altogether?

Date: _____

 To multiply a two-digit number by a one-digit number, follow these steps.

1. *Multiply the ones digit.*   2. *Multiply the tens digit.*

$$4 \times 2 = 8 \quad \begin{array}{r} 34 \\ \times\ 2 \\ \hline 8 \end{array}$$ $$3 \times 2 = 6 \quad \begin{array}{r} 34 \\ \times\ 2 \\ \hline 68 \end{array}$$

Multiply. Then use the code to answer the riddle below.

$$\begin{array}{r} 23 \\ \times\ 2 \\ \hline \end{array}$$
U

$$\begin{array}{r} 12 \\ \times\ 3 \\ \hline \end{array}$$
A

$$\begin{array}{r} 14 \\ \times\ 2 \\ \hline \end{array}$$
Q

$$\begin{array}{r} 31 \\ \times\ 3 \\ \hline \end{array}$$
E

$$\begin{array}{r} 33 \\ \times\ 3 \\ \hline \end{array}$$
E

$$\begin{array}{r} 71 \\ \times\ 3 \\ \hline \end{array}$$
J

$$\begin{array}{r} 83 \\ \times\ 2 \\ \hline \end{array}$$
D

$$\begin{array}{r} 22 \\ \times\ 4 \\ \hline \end{array}$$
!

$$\begin{array}{r} 24 \\ \times\ 2 \\ \hline \end{array}$$
C

$$\begin{array}{r} 11 \\ \times\ 5 \\ \hline \end{array}$$
N

$$\begin{array}{r} 43 \\ \times\ 3 \\ \hline \end{array}$$
A

$$\begin{array}{r} 74 \\ \times\ 2 \\ \hline \end{array}$$
S

$$\begin{array}{r} 52 \\ \times\ 4 \\ \hline \end{array}$$
R

$$\begin{array}{r} 33 \\ \times\ 2 \\ \hline \end{array}$$
S

What kind of dancers are math teachers?

___ ___ ___ ___ ___ ___
66 28 46 129 208 99

___ ___ ___ ___ ___ ___ ___ ___
166 36 55 48 93 208 148 88

Date: _____

Multiply. Time yourself to see how fast you can finish the race.

$$24 \times 2$$

$$51 \times 5$$

$$92 \times 4$$

$$63 \times 2$$

$$14 \times 2$$

$$12 \times 4$$

$$73 \times 3$$

$$83 \times 2$$

$$44 \times 2$$

$$61 \times 4$$

$$51 \times 2$$

$$42 \times 3$$

 Three race cars raced around the track. Each race car completed 32 laps. How many laps in all did the race cars complete?

Date: _____

Multiply.

1.
$$314 \times 2$$
$$230 \times 3$$

2.
$$432 \times 3$$
$$521 \times 4$$

3.
$$604 \times 2$$
$$702 \times 3$$

4.
$$723 \times 3$$
$$921 \times 2$$
$$241 \times 2$$
$$813 \times 3$$

5.
$$112 \times 3$$
$$124 \times 2$$
$$303 \times 3$$
$$620 \times 4$$

The school science lab has 3 sets of test tubes. Each set has 112 tubes. How many are there in all?

Date: _____

Multiply. Color an apple if you find its product.

1.
   203
   ×   3

   411
   ×   2

   310
   ×   1

   212
   ×   3

2.
   110
   ×   7

   141
   ×   2

   130
   ×   3

   302
   ×   3

3.
   114
   ×   2

   524
   ×   1

   333
   ×   3

   230
   ×   2

310   770   460   609

282

812   906   999   390   656

228   524

 There are 4 crates of apples to unpack. If each crate has 102 apples, how many apples are there altogether?

Date: _____

 Sometimes regrouping will be needed when multiplying with a two-digit number. Follow these steps to solve the problem.

1. Multiply the ones. Regroup if needed.

$7 \times 6 = 42$

$$\begin{array}{r} 4 \\ 47 \\ \times\ 6 \\ \hline 2 \end{array}$$

2. Multiply the tens. Add the extra tens.

$4 \times 6 = 24$

$24 + 4 = 28$

$$\begin{array}{r} 4 \\ 47 \\ \times\ 6 \\ \hline 282 \end{array}$$

Multiply. Remember to regroup.

1. $\begin{array}{r} 36 \\ \times\ 4 \\ \hline \end{array}$ $\begin{array}{r} 25 \\ \times\ 5 \\ \hline \end{array}$ $\begin{array}{r} 63 \\ \times\ 7 \\ \hline \end{array}$

2. $\begin{array}{r} 83 \\ \times\ 8 \\ \hline \end{array}$ $\begin{array}{r} 72 \\ \times\ 6 \\ \hline \end{array}$ $\begin{array}{r} 29 \\ \times\ 4 \\ \hline \end{array}$ $\begin{array}{r} 47 \\ \times\ 6 \\ \hline \end{array}$ $\begin{array}{r} 55 \\ \times\ 7 \\ \hline \end{array}$

3. $\begin{array}{r} 62 \\ \times\ 5 \\ \hline \end{array}$ $\begin{array}{r} 96 \\ \times\ 2 \\ \hline \end{array}$ $\begin{array}{r} 58 \\ \times\ 5 \\ \hline \end{array}$ $\begin{array}{r} 49 \\ \times\ 3 \\ \hline \end{array}$ $\begin{array}{r} 96 \\ \times\ 4 \\ \hline \end{array}$

Date: _____

Multiply. Regroup inside each leaf. Then use the code to answer the riddle below.

N 34
× 6

C 17
× 3

A 46
× 4

H 62
× 5

I 53
× 6

B 72
× 7

S 28
× 4

K 48
× 2

R 18
× 6

B 39
× 3

Where does a tree keep its money?

—— ——   —— —— —— —— —— ——   —— —— —— —— ——!
318 204   117 108 184 204 51 310   504 184 204 96 112

Date: _____

Multiply. Remember to regroup if needed.

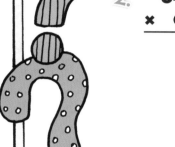

1.
53	63	46	73
× 3	× 2	× 4	× 4

2.
34	82	35	27
× 6	× 4	× 5	× 4

3.
75	23	52	32
× 2	× 7	× 3	× 2

4.
29	38	48	84
× 2	× 5	× 6	× 2

 Circle each problem above that did not need regrouping. Is there a pattern?

Date: _____

hot dog
72¢

popcorn
29¢

pretzel
68¢

soda
95¢

snow cone
43¢

cotton
candy   87¢

Write a multiplication sentence for each problem. Multiply.

1. What is the cost of 4 hot dogs?

   _____ × _____ = _____ ¢

2. How much will 6 bags of popcorn cost?

   _____ × _____ = _____ ¢

3. If you buy 3 pretzels, how much will you spend?

   _____ × _____ = _____ ¢

4. What is the cost of 3 cotton candies?

   _____ × _____ = _____ ¢

5. What is the cost of 2 snow cones and 2 popcorns?

   _____ × _____ = _____ ¢

   _____ × _____ = _____ ¢

   _____ + _____ = _____ ¢

6. You bought 3 sodas and 2 pretzels. How much did you spend?

   _____ × _____ = _____ ¢

   _____ × _____ = _____ ¢

   _____ + _____ = _____ ¢

 On another sheet of paper, write a multiplication word problem using the prices of the snacks above. Solve.

Date: _____

 To multiply with a 2-digit factor that requires regrouping, follow these steps.

1. Multiply by the ones digit.

$$
\begin{array}{r}
3 \\
46 \\
\times\ 26 \\
\hline
276
\end{array}
$$

2. Place a zero in the ones column.

$$
\begin{array}{r}
3 \\
46 \\
\times\ 26 \\
\hline
276 \\
0
\end{array}
$$

3. Multiply by the tens digit.

$$
\begin{array}{r}
3 \\
46 \\
\times\ 26 \\
\hline
276 \\
+\ 920
\end{array}
$$

4. Add to find the product.

$$
\begin{array}{r}
1 \\
3 \\
46 \\
\times\ 26 \\
\hline
276 \\
+\ 920 \\
\hline
1,196
\end{array}
$$

Multiply. Then use the code to answer the riddle below.

32 × 48	67 × 14	53 × 27	96 × 52	83 × 33	49 × 72
G	**T**	**S**	**I**	**A**	**D**
39 × 28	56 × 15	83 × 24	75 × 46	96 × 51	84 × 62
M	**E**	**N**	**R**	**K**	**H**

What horses like to stay up late?

_____ _____ _____ _____ _____ _____ _____ _____ _____ _____ !

1,992 4,992 1,536 5,208 938 1,092 2,739 3,450 840 1,431

 Each of Farmer Gray's 24 horses eat 68 kg of hay. How many kg of hay do the horses eat altogether?

Date: _____

Solve the problems. If the answer is even, connect the dot beside each problem to the heart on the right- and left-hand sides of the circle. If the answer is odd, do nothing. Two lines have been drawn for you.

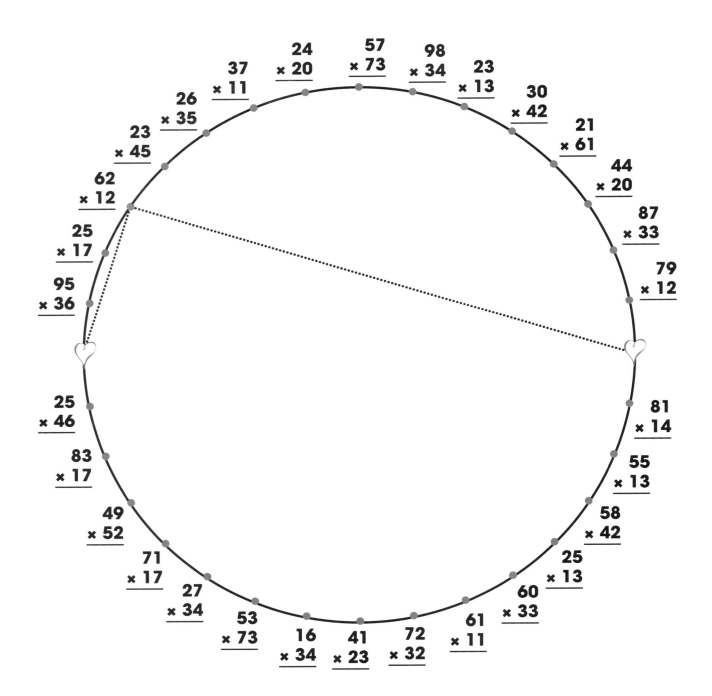

Date: _____

Multiply. Then use a calculator to check your work.

1. 315
    × 9

2. 456
    × 4

3. 675
    × 5

4. 764
    × 7

5. 219
    × 8

6. 968
    × 3

7. 391
    × 4

8. 532
    × 6

9. 808
    × 4

10. 270
    × 9

On another piece of paper, write five multiplication problems with a three-digit number. Multiply. Check each answer with a calculator.

Date: _____

Multiply. If the ones digit in the product is less than five, mark an O in the box. If the ones digit is five or greater, mark an X. Are there three in a row?

Game 1

56 × 7	129 × 8	42 × 3
238 × 3	251 × 6	132 × 4
62 × 4	83 × 4	185 × 2

Game 2

97 × 3	189 × 4	224 × 4
76 × 4	55 × 8	252 × 3
225 × 4	304 × 2	58 × 3

On another sheet of paper, make up your own multiplication tic-tac-toe game.

Date: _____

To make easy numbers, first multiply numbers that result in either 10 or 100. Then multiply the rest of the numbers in the equation. For example:

$$2 \times 9 \times 5$$
$$= (2 \times 5) \times 9$$
$$= 10 \times 9$$
$$= 90$$

Make easy numbers to solve the problems below. Draw a line to match the problem to the answer.

1. **2 × 9 × 5 = _____**   •   • **300**

2. **10 × 3 × 10 = _____**   •   • **800**

3. **5 × 13 × 2 = _____**   •   • **250**

4. **2 × 5 × 37 = _____**   •   • **600**

5. **50 × 7 × 2 = _____**   •   • **700**

6. **4 × 8 × 25 = _____**   •   • **90**

7. **50 × 9 × 2 = _____**   •   • **500**

8. **5 × 5 × 5 × 2 = _____** •   • **370**

9. **2 × 2 × 5 × 3 = _____** •   • **60**

10. **2 × 10 × 5 × 5 = _____** •   • **900**

11. **1 × 2 × 4 × 2 × 5 = _____** •   • **130**

12. **2 × 3 × 5 × 4 × 5 = _____** •   • **80**

Date: _____

Write a number sentence for each problem on pages 40 and 41. Solve.

1. Connor's dog, Barky, made 3 holes in the backyard. Connor's dad had to fill each hole with 78 scoops of dirt. How many scoops did his dad need in all?

2. Barky got into Steve's closet. He chewed up 8 pairs of shoes. How many shoes did he chew altogether?

3. Adrienne went to the store to buy doggie treats. She bought 6 boxes of doggie treats. Each box has 48 treats. How many treats in all did Adrienne buy?

 On another piece of paper, write your own Barky word problem. Solve.

4. Terri took Barky to the vet for 3 shots. Each shot cost $265. How much money did Terri pay the vet?

5. Max's job is to keep Barky's water bowl full. If he fills it 3 times a day for 24 days, how many times did he fill the bowl altogether?

6. Barky runs around the block 4 times every day. How many times does he run around the block in 5 days?

 Write more Barky word problems. Solve.

Date: _____

To divide means to make equal groups. The total number being divided is called the **dividend**. *The number of groups the total is to be divided into is called the* **divisor**. *The answer is called the* **quotient**. $6 \div 2 = 3$

| total number (dividend–6) | number of groups (divisor–2) | number in each group (quotient–3) |

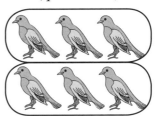

Solve the following problems by drawing a picture. Draw the number of birds you think need to go in each cage. (Hint: Each cage must have the same number of birds.) Then complete the number sentence.

1. The Bird House has 10 birds in all. The zookeeper wants to put the birds into the 5 new cages he bought. How many birds will he put in each cage?

Total Number of Birds	**Number of Cages**	**Number of Birds in Each Cage**
_____ $\div$	5 =	_____

2. What if the zookeeper only had 2 cages? How many birds would go in each cage?

_____ $\div$ _____ = _____

Date: _____

Draw a circle around the correct number of stars to show each division problem. Complete each number sentence.

1. 8 ÷ 2 = ___4___

2. 6 ÷ 3 = _____

3. 12 ÷ 3 = _____

4. 10 ÷ 2 = _____

5. 18 ÷ 3 = _____

6. 9 ÷ 3 = _____

7. 16 ÷ 2 = _____

8. 15 ÷ 3 = _____

Date: _____

Divide.

1. 6 ÷ 2 = _____   9 ÷ 3 = _____   10 ÷ 2 = _____

2. 12 ÷ 3 = _____   14 ÷ 2 = _____   8 ÷ 2 = _____

3. 2 ÷ 2 = _____   18 ÷ 3 = _____   24 ÷ 3 = _____

4. 2)‾12‾   3)‾21‾

5. 3)‾6‾   3)‾3‾

6. 3)‾15‾   2)‾16‾

 There are 18 aliens ready to board their spaceships. If 6 aliens get on each spaceship, how many spaceships do they need? Draw a picture to show the problem. Then write a number sentence to solve the problem.

Date: _____

You can use a number line to help divide. Count back in equal groups to 0.

$$28 \div 4 = 7$$

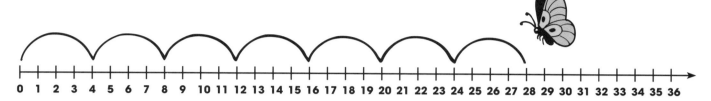

Divide. Use the number line to help you.

1. $4\overline{)16}$ $4\overline{)36}$ $4\overline{)4}$ $4\overline{)24}$

2. $4\overline{)20}$ $4\overline{)12}$ $4\overline{)32}$ $4\overline{)8}$

3. $32 \div 4 =$ _____ $16 \div 4 =$ _____ $20 \div 4 =$ _____

Divide. Use the number line to help you.

4. $5\overline{)15}$ $5\overline{)5}$ $5\overline{)40}$ $5\overline{)45}$

5. $5\overline{)25}$ $5\overline{)10}$ $5\overline{)20}$ $5\overline{)10}$

Date: _____

Divide.

1. 30 ÷ 5 = _____   32 ÷ 4 = _____   45 ÷ 5 = _____   5 ÷ 5 = _____

2. 36 ÷ 4 = _____   20 ÷ 4 = _____   25 ÷ 5 = _____   28 ÷ 4 = _____

3. 5)‾10‾   4)‾16‾   5)‾40‾   5)‾45‾   4)‾20‾

4. 4)‾12‾   5)‾35‾   4)‾8‾   5)‾15‾   4)‾24‾

5. Lisa tied a total of 12 ribbons on her kites.
   If she tied 4 ribbons on each kite,
   how many kites does Lisa have?   _____ ÷ _____ = _____

There were **36 people flying kites in the park. There were an equal number of yellow, green, orange and blue kites. How many kites are there of each color?**

Date: _____

Divide.

1. 42 ÷ 7 = _____   54 ÷ 6 = _____   36 ÷ 6 = _____

2. 24 ÷ 6 = _____   63 ÷ 7 = _____   48 ÷ 6 = _____

3. 14 ÷ 7 = _____   56 ÷ 7 = _____   28 ÷ 7 = _____

4. 49 ÷ 7 = _____   60 ÷ 6 = _____   42 ÷ 6 = _____

5. Fifty-six students went on a field trip to the zoo. They traveled in 7 vans. How many students were in each van?

MONKEY HOUSE

6. When the students went to the monkey house, they found it was divided into 6 rooms. The same number of monkeys were in each room. There were 24 monkeys in all. How many monkeys were in each room?

Date: _____

Divide.

1. 6)30   7)28   6)12   6)48

2. 7)49   6)18   7)35   6)6

3. 21 ÷ 7 = _____   7 ÷ 7 = _____   42 ÷ 6 = _____

4. 14 ÷ 7 = _____   24 ÷ 6 = _____   36 ÷ 6 = _____

5. **Divide by 6**

0	6	12	18	24	30	36	42	48	54

6. **Divide by 7**

0	7	14	21	28	35	42	49	56	63

 Circle the division number sentence above that shows the picture of the frogs on the lily pads. On another sheet of paper, write a word problem using another number sentence from above.

Date: _____

Divide to find the answers on each runner's path to the finish line.

$81 \div 9 =$ _____

$16 \div 8 =$ _____

$32 \div 8 =$ _____

$45 \div 9 =$ _____

$8\overline{)40}$

$9\overline{)63}$

$64 \div 8 =$ _____

$18 \div 9 =$ _____

$27 \div 9 =$ _____

$9 \div 9 =$ _____

$9\overline{)36}$

$8\overline{)24}$

$9\overline{)54}$

$8\overline{)72}$

FINISH

$0 \div 8 =$ _____

$56 \div 8 =$ _____

$48 \div 8 =$ _____

$80 \div 8 =$ _____

 Last week in track practice, Andy ran 36 km. He ran the same number of kilometers on each of the 4 days. How many kilometers did he run each day?

Date: _____

Circle the skates and helmets with the correct quotient.

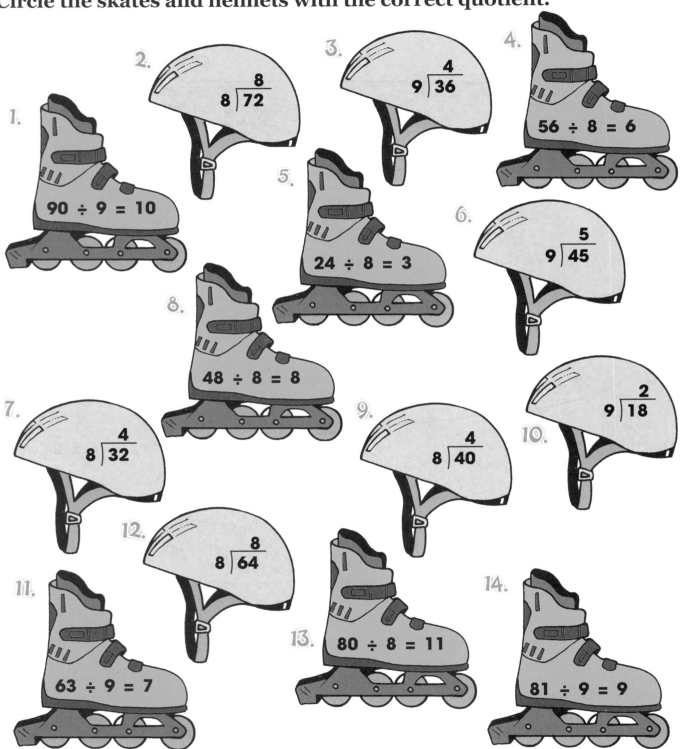

2. $8\overline{)72}$ → 8

3. $9\overline{)36}$ → 4

4. $56 \div 8 = 6$

1. $90 \div 9 = 10$

5. $24 \div 8 = 3$

6. $9\overline{)45}$ → 5

8. $48 \div 8 = 8$

7. $8\overline{)32}$ → 4

9. $8\overline{)40}$ → 4

10. $9\overline{)18}$ → 2

12. $8\overline{)64}$ → 8

11. $63 \div 9 = 7$

13. $80 \div 8 = 11$

14. $81 \div 9 = 9$

Peter wants to skate 18 km in the next 9 days. If he skates an equal number of kilometers each day, how many kilometers will he need to skate each day?

Use these steps when dividing with greater dividends.

1. Divide the tens digit in the dividend by the divisor. Write the answer above the tens digit.

$$\begin{array}{r} 2 \\ 4\overline{)84} \end{array}$$

2. Multiply the partial quotient by the divisor. Write the answer below the tens digit. Subtract. Bring down the ones digit.

$$\begin{array}{r} 2 \\ 4\overline{)84} \\ -8\downarrow \\ \hline 04 \end{array}$$

3. Divide the ones digit by the divisor. Write the answer above the ones digit. Multiply. Subtract.

$$\begin{array}{r} 21 \\ 4\overline{)84} \\ -8\downarrow \\ \hline 04 \\ -4 \\ \hline 0 \end{array}$$

Divide.

1. $3\overline{)66}$ $2\overline{)48}$ $3\overline{)93}$ $3\overline{)39}$

2. $3\overline{)96}$ $3\overline{)63}$ $2\overline{)68}$ $9\overline{)90}$

3. $3\overline{)99}$ $3\overline{)69}$ $2\overline{)80}$ $5\overline{)55}$

Date: _____

 Remember to follow each step when dividing larger numbers.

1. Divide the tens digit by the divisor. Multiply. Subtract.

$$\begin{array}{r} 1 \\ 3\overline{)45} \\ -3 \\ \hline 1 \end{array}$$

2. Bring down the ones digit. Divide this number by the divisor.

$$\begin{array}{r} 15 \\ 3\overline{)45} \\ -3\downarrow \\ \hline 15 \end{array}$$

3. Multiply. Subtract.

$$\begin{array}{r} 15 \\ 3\overline{)45} \\ -3\downarrow \\ \hline 15 \\ -15 \\ \hline 0 \end{array}$$

Divide.

1. $2\overline{)58}$ $5\overline{)85}$ $6\overline{)72}$ $5\overline{)90}$

2. $3\overline{)48}$ $8\overline{)96}$ $2\overline{)74}$ $4\overline{)92}$

3. $6\overline{)78}$ $4\overline{)76}$ $5\overline{)65}$ $4\overline{)60}$

 Andrew has 87 marbles. He divides them into 3 bags. How many marbles are in each bag? Solve. Then circle the problem above with the same quotient.

Date: _____

Sometimes when you try to divide a number into equal groups, part of the number is left over. This is called the **remainder**. Use these steps to find the remainder.

1.
$$5\overline{)16}$$

Think: 5 × __ is the closest to 16?

2.
$$\begin{array}{r} 3 \\ 5\overline{)16} \\ -15 \\ \hline 1 \end{array}$$

3.
$$\begin{array}{r} 3\ R\ 1 \\ 5\overline{)16} \\ -15 \\ \hline 1 \end{array}$$

There are 5 groups of 3 with 1 left over.

Divide.

1.
$$\begin{array}{r} 1\ R4 \\ 6\overline{)10} \\ -6 \\ \hline 4 \end{array}$$
$$2\overline{)9}$$

2. $3\overline{)20}$ $2\overline{)19}$ $6\overline{)47}$ $6\overline{)41}$

3. $7\overline{)51}$ $2\overline{)15}$ $3\overline{)22}$ $7\overline{)48}$

4. $2\overline{)11}$ $4\overline{)26}$ $6\overline{)19}$ $5\overline{)27}$

 Louie jumps hurdles for his track meet. He jumps the same number in each race. In his last 6 races, he jumped 36 hurdles. How many hurdles did he jump each day?

Date: _____

Divide.

1. 5)41   6)52   3)19   8)74

2. 4)29   2)13   7)38   9)46

3. 5)21   6)31   3)26   8)57

4. 4)14   2)7   7)65   9)51

5. 3)13   6)39   5)14   8)50

 Candy's mom bought 56 apples to make 8 pies. If she used an equal number of apples in each pie, how many apples did she use in each pie? Solve on another piece of paper.

Date: _____

 To divide with remainders, follow these steps.

1. Does $8 \times$ __ = 34?
   No!

   $8 \overline{)34}$

2. Use the closest smaller dividend.
   $8 \times 4 = 32$

   $\begin{array}{r} 4 \\ 8\overline{)34} \\ 32 \end{array}$

3. Subtract to find the remainder.

   $\begin{array}{r} 4 \\ 8\overline{)34} \\ -32 \\ \hline 2 \end{array}$

4. The remainder is always less than the divisor.

   $\begin{array}{r} 4\,R2 \\ 8\overline{)34} \\ -32 \\ \hline 2 \end{array}$

Divide. Then use the code to complete the riddle below.

E $9\overline{)84}$ L $3\overline{)29}$ S $7\overline{)67}$ O $5\overline{)24}$

T $6\overline{)23}$ N $6\overline{)47}$ P $6\overline{)40}$ I $7\overline{)52}$

O $4\overline{)19}$ A $8\overline{)70}$ T $3\overline{)26}$ S $9\overline{)55}$

H $4\overline{)23}$! $7\overline{)45}$ R $5\overline{)27}$ N $8\overline{)79}$

Emily: Yesterday I saw a man at the mall with very long arms.
         Every time he went up the stairs he stepped on them.

Jack: Wow! He stepped on his arms?

Emily: ____ ____ ,   ____ ____   ____ ____ ____
         7 R5 4 R4   4 R3 9 R7   8 R2 5 R3 9 R3

         ____ ____ ____ ____ ____ ____ ____
         9 R4 3 R5 8 R6 7 R3 5 R2 6 R1 6 R3

Date: _____

Steve works in a candy store. He puts candy into boxes. Each box has 10 spaces. Steve has 32 candies. Try to draw 32 candies in the boxes below. Write the number of candies in each box on the line.

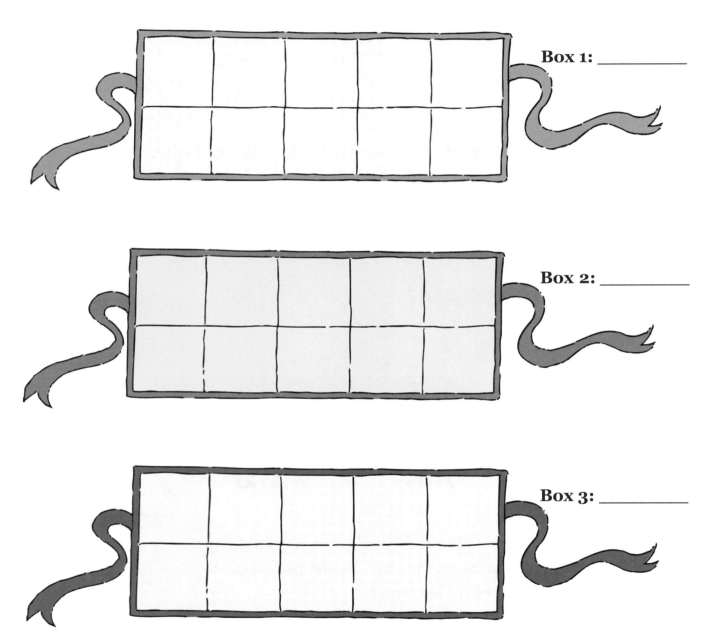

Box 1: _____

Box 2: _____

Box 3: _____

Write the number of any leftover candy. _____ .

Find each quotient. Then use the code to solve the riddle by filling in the blanks at the bottom of the page.

I	8
L	3 remainder 2
W	7
S	8 remainder 1
U	6
A	9
B	15 remainder 3
L	4
D	2 remainder 3
T	9 remainder 2
F	1
N	7 remainder 6
I	6 remainder 6
E	2
O	11
P	15 remainder 2
X	2 remainder 5
C	10
R	5

1. $8 \div 2 =$ _____

2. $10 \div 5 =$ _____

3. $24 \div 4 =$ _____

4. $50 \div 10 =$ _____

5. $72 \div 9 =$ _____

6. $32 \div 10 =$ _____

7. $48 \div 7 =$ _____

8. $29 \div 3 =$ _____

9. $65 \div 8 =$ _____

10. $92 \div 6 =$ _____

What kind of tools do you use for math?

"M ___ ___ ___ ___" ___ ___ ___ ___ ___
    3   1   8   5   10 6 7 2 4 9

Remember that multiplication and division are related. Multiplying the quotient by the divisor will tell you the dividend.

Hi! Aren't we related?

You bet! When you multiply us, our missing product is the missing dividend!

Write each missing dividend.

1. _____ ÷ 9 = 7   _____ ÷ 4 = 6   _____ ÷ 6 = 6   _____ ÷ 5 = 7

2. _____ ÷ 3 = 3   _____ ÷ 2 = 9   _____ ÷ 8 = 6   _____ ÷ 9 = 9

3. _____ ÷ 4 = 8   _____ ÷ 3 = 7   _____ ÷ 2 = 8   _____ ÷ 6 = 3

4. _____ ÷ 8 = 8   _____ ÷ 1 = 9   _____ ÷ 5 = 6   _____ ÷ 7 = 1

Are we missing?

5. _____ ÷ 4 = 40   _____ ÷ 3 = 30   _____ ÷ 3 = 100

6. _____ ÷ 7 = 60   _____ ÷ 5 = 60   _____ ÷ 2 = 40

 At our family reunion picnic, 8 people sat at each picnic table. We needed 16 tables. How many people altogether were at the reunion?

Date: _____

Remember: The **quotient** *tells how many equal groups you can make. The* **remainder** *tells how many are left over.*

Divide. Answer each question.

1. A clothing-store clerk has 14 sweaters. He wants to put them in equal stacks on 3 shelves. How many sweaters will be in each stack?

2. Mary has 57¢. She wants to buy candy canes that cost 9¢ each. How many candy canes can she buy?

3. Rosa needs to bake 71 cookies. Each cookie sheet holds 8 cookies. How many cookies are on the unfilled cookie sheet?

Divide. Answer each question.

4. There are 17 cars waiting to be parked, but not enough parking spaces. There are an equal number of parking spots on 3 different levels. How many cars will not find a parking spot?

5. Luis is putting 74 cans into cartons. Each carton holds 8 cans. How many cans will be in the unfilled carton?

6. Don bought 85 crates of flowers. He separates them into groups of 9. How many equal groups did he have?

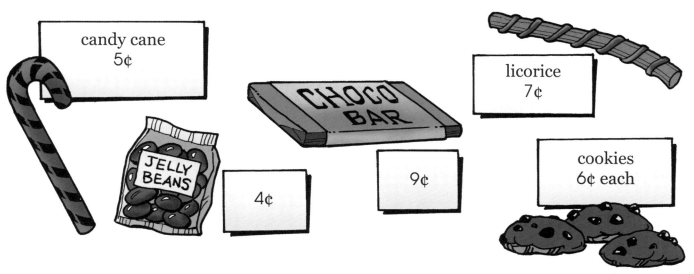

Write a number sentence for each problem. Solve.

1. Suzanne has 96¢. How many cookies can she buy?

2. Lee has 98¢. How many chocolate bars can she buy? How much money will she have left over?

3. Jose has 72¢. How many bags of jelly beans can he buy?

4. Connie has 84¢. How many cookies can she buy?

5. Toby is in the mood for candy canes. How many can he buy with 63¢?

6. Ann is buying licorice for her friends. How many pieces can she buy for 74¢? What could she buy with the remaining money?

 The price of which item above can divide $1.00 evenly?

Date: _____

*Multiplication is the opposite of division. The product and factors can be used to write division sentences. The multiplication and division sentences are called a **fact family**.*

$2 \times 6 = 12$ *(2 groups of 6)* $12 \div 6 = 2$ *(12 divided into 6 equal groups)*

$6 \times 2 = 12$ *(6 groups of 2)* $12 \div 2 = 6$ *(12 divided into 2 equal groups)*

Write two multiplication and two division sentences for each set of numbers.

1. **2, 3, 6**

_____

_____

_____

_____

2. **2, 8, 16**

_____

_____

_____

_____

3. **4, 5, 20**

_____

_____

_____

_____

4. **3, 5, 15**

_____

_____

_____

_____

5. **3, 9, 27**

_____

_____

_____

_____

6. **3, 12, 36**

_____

_____

_____

_____

7. **5, 6, 30**

_____

_____

_____

_____

8. **6, 7, 42**

_____

_____

_____

_____

9. **4, 8, 32**

_____

_____

_____

_____

 Ramone has 33 marbles. He keeps an equal number of marbles in each of 3 bags. How many marbles are in each bag? On another piece of paper, write a number sentence to solve this problem. Then write the set of numbers in this fact family.

Date: _____

Division is the opposite of multiplication. The dividend, divisor and quotient can be used to write multiplication sentences. The division and multiplication sentences are called a **fact family.**

$15 \div 3 = 5$ *(15 divided into 3 equal groups)*
$15 \div 5 = 3$ *(15 divided into 5 equal groups)*
$3 \times 5 = 15$ *(3 groups of 5)*
$5 \times 3 = 15$ *(5 groups of 3)*

Use the numbers from each fish family to write fact family number sentences.

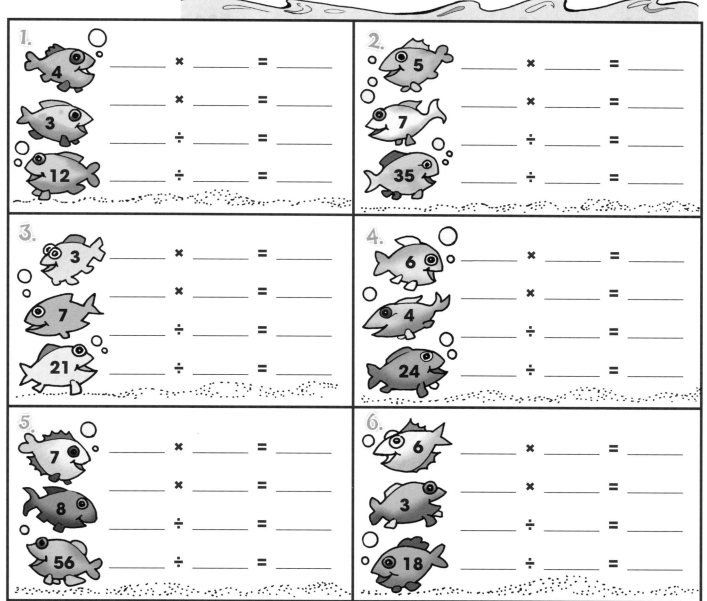

1. 4 3 12

_____ × _____ = _____

_____ × _____ = _____

_____ ÷ _____ = _____

_____ ÷ _____ = _____

2. 5 7 35

_____ × _____ = _____

_____ × _____ = _____

_____ ÷ _____ = _____

_____ ÷ _____ = _____

3. 3 7 21

_____ × _____ = _____

_____ × _____ = _____

_____ ÷ _____ = _____

_____ ÷ _____ = _____

4. 6 4 24

_____ × _____ = _____

_____ × _____ = _____

_____ ÷ _____ = _____

_____ ÷ _____ = _____

5. 7 8 56

_____ × _____ = _____

_____ × _____ = _____

_____ ÷ _____ = _____

_____ ÷ _____ = _____

6. 6 3 18

_____ × _____ = _____

_____ × _____ = _____

_____ ÷ _____ = _____

_____ ÷ _____ = _____

Date: _____

 To multiply with zeros, follow these steps.

| 90 | 9 × 2 = 18 |
| × 2 | Add a zero in the ones place to make 180. |

| 90 | 9 × 2 = 18 |
| × 20 | Add 2 zeros — one in the ones place and one in the tens place. |

| 900 | 9 × 2 = 18 |
| × 20 | Add 3 zeros — one in the ones place, one in the tens place and one in the hundreds place. |

Multiply.

1.

80	60	900	40	120	200
× 7	× 50	× 30	× 11	× 2	× 60

2.

70	120	60	700	50	30
× 7	× 300	× 90	× 60	× 70	× 12

3.

600	40	30	90	200	50
× 80	× 12	× 8	× 50	× 120	× 8

To divide with zeros, follow these samples.

$$8\overline{)640} = 80 \qquad \begin{array}{l} 64 \div 8 = 8 \\ 0 \div 8 = 0 \\ \text{Add a zero to} \\ \text{make 80.} \end{array}$$

$$8\overline{)6400} = 800 \qquad \begin{array}{l} 64 \div 8 = 8 \\ 0 \div 8 = 0 \\ 0 \div 8 = 0 \\ \text{Add 2 zeros} \\ \text{to make 800.} \end{array}$$

Divide.

1. $6\overline{)420}$ $9\overline{)8100}$ $6\overline{)540}$ $5\overline{)4500}$ $3\overline{)2400}$

2. $3\overline{)1800}$ $4\overline{)320}$ $8\overline{)7200}$ $7\overline{)560}$ $5\overline{)400}$

3. $3\overline{)150}$ $4\overline{)360}$ $6\overline{)4800}$ $6\overline{)360}$ $8\overline{)640}$

Date: _____

 The order of the factors in a multiplication sentence can change without changing the value of the product. If 2 × 7 is changed to 7 × 2, the product still equals 14.

Change the order of the factors in each multiplication sentence.

1. **6 × 2 = 12**

_____

2. **4 × 8 = 32**

_____

3. **3 × 9 = 27**

_____

4. **3 × 7 = 21**

_____

5. **5 × 9 = 45**

_____

6. **6 × 7 = 42**

_____

7. **7 × 4 = 28**

_____

8. **3 × 12 = 36**

_____

9. **9 × 8 = 72**

_____

10. **6 × 5 = 30**

_____

11. **4 × 10 = 40**

_____

12. **9 × 7 = 63**

_____

13. **2 × 11 = 22**

_____

14. **12 × 11 = 132**

_____

Solve each problem by breaking up numbers. Then regroup the numbers for easier multiplication and division. Look at the multiplication and division examples here.

> ### Example
>
> 3×56
> $= 3 \times (50 + 6)$
> $= (3 \times 50) + (3 \times 6)$
> $= 150 + 18$
> $= 168$
>
> $36 \div 4$
> $= (20 + 16) \div 4$
> $= (20 \div 4) + (16 \div 4)$
> $= 5 + 4$
> $= 9$

1. $3 \times 12 = $ _____

2. $5 \times 31 = $ _____

3. $4 \times 62 = $ _____

4. $2 \times 43 = $ _____

5. $8 \times 13 = $ _____

6. $6 \times 36 = $ _____

7. $24 \div 4 = $ _____

8. $35 \div 5 = $ _____

9. $48 \div 8 = $ _____

10. $56 \div 7 = $ _____

11. $96 \div 8 = $ _____

12. $64 \div 4 = $ _____

Date: _____

Decide whether to multiply or divide. Solve.

1. Ellen baked 75 cookies in 3 hours. Joe baked 96 cookies in 4 hours. Who baked the most cookies per hour?

2. James pitched 18 times in each inning of the ball game. How many times did he pitch in the 9 innings?

3. Lana bought sixty 20 ml sodas. How many 60 ml servings can she give her party guests?

Decide whether to multiply or divide. Solve.

4. Cory's mom sent him to the store for eggs. He bought 4 cartons of a dozen eggs. How many eggs did he purchase in all?

5. Maria made bracelets for her friends. She put 9 beads on each. She had 81 beads. How many bracelets did she make?

6. It costs 50¢ per hour to park at the beach. How much did it cost David's parents to park for 8 hours?

Fill in the bubble next to the correct answer.

1. 333
  × 3

- ○ **A** 999
- ○ **B** 989
- ○ **C** 987
- ○ **D** 936

3. 125
  × 7

- ○ **A** 875
- ○ **B** 775
- ○ **C** 735
- ○ **D** 835

2. Find the missing factor.

4 × _____ = 12

- ○ **A** 3
- ○ **B** 4
- ○ **C** 5
- ○ **D** 6

4. Find the missing factor.

_____ × 9 = 18

- ○ **A** 4
- ○ **B** 2
- ○ **C** 3
- ○ **D** 5

Fill in the bubble next to the correct answer.

5. $65 \div 5 =$

- ○ **A** 11
- ○ **B** 12
- ○ **C** 13
- ○ **D** 14

7. $8\overline{)16}$

- ○ **A** 5
- ○ **B** 4
- ○ **C** 3
- ○ **D** 2

6. $16 \div 4 =$

- ○ **A** 1
- ○ **B** 3
- ○ **C** 4
- ○ **D** 5

8. $5\overline{)40}$

- ○ **A** 6
- ○ **B** 7
- ○ **C** 8
- ○ **D** 9

Fill in the bubble next to the correct answer.

9. Forty-eight students went on a field trip to the zoo. They traveled in 6 vans. How many students were in each van?

◯ **A**   7   ◯ **B**   8

◯ **C**   5   ◯ **D**   9

10. When the students went to the snake house they found 5 cages. There were 4 snakes in each cage. How many snakes were in the snake house?

◯ **A**   30   ◯ **B**   25

◯ **C**   20   ◯ **D**   35

11. When the students went to see the lions, they saw 3 separate cages. There were 2 lions in each cage. How many lions were in the lion house?

◯ **A**   6   ◯ **B**   3

◯ **C**   2   ◯ **D**   4

Read the questions. Write the number sentence for each question and solve the problem.

12. Katie saves $47 every week. How much does she save in 22 weeks?

13. Mom uses 200 g of flour to bake a sponge cake. How much flour does Mom need to bake 5 such cakes?

14. Each child has 4 pencils. There are 80 children. How many pencils are there in all?

Read the questions. Write the number sentence for each question and solve the problem.

15. There are 50 lucky draw coupons. Each family has 5 coupons. How many families are there?

16. There are 81 marshmallows. Each child eats 9 marshmallows. How many children are there?

17. Mom bought 72 eggs. She put 6 eggs in each carton. How many cartons did Mom use?

Answer Key

Page 6
1. 4, 9, 12
2. 12, 18, 21
3. 14, 18, 10
4. 2, 24, 10, 0, 6, 14
5. 8, 9, 3, 12, 0, 3

Page 7
Review models.
1. 3 × 3 = 9 points
2. 4 × 2 = 8 hockey sticks

Page 8
Review arrays.
1. 12   2. 30   3. 10
4. 24   5. 32   6. 15

Page 9
Review grids.
1. (3, 4), 12   2. (2, 4), 8
3. (3, 2), 6   4. (1, 5), 5
5. (5, 2), 10   6. (3, 6), 18

Page 10
Across	Down
2. thirty-six	1. sixteen
4. twenty	2. thirty-two
7. twelve	3. forty-eight
8. twenty-eight	5. eight
9. forty	6. twenty-four
11. zero	10. four
12. forty-four;	

44 buttons

Page 11
1. 10   2. 1   3. 7   4. 50
5. 12   6. 30   7. 11   8. 15
9. 40   10. 9   11. 5   12. 5
13. 35   14. 60   15. 4;   48 nuts

Page 12
B. 12	R. 4	A. 8	F. 32
P. 28	S. 30	U. 15	E. 5
U. 16	I. 25	G. 0	S. 10
O. 20	D. 45	I. 36	N. 24
S. 35	C. 40;		

SIRIUS and CANOPUS

Page 13

36 km

Page 14
1. 36, 14   2. 7, 30   3. 12, 28
4. 0, 49   5. 42, 12, 63, 24, 36, 21
6. 18, 56, 6, 35, 54, 42;
4 × 7 = 28 flowers

Page 15
Across	Down
1. forty-five	2. twenty-seven
5. nine	3. fifty-four
7. one hundred eight	4. zero
9. thirty-six	6. seventy-two
10. ninety	8. sixty-three
12. eighteen	11. eighty-one
13. ninety-nine;	

Page 16

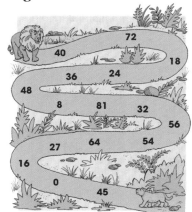

16 cubs

Page 17
1. 54, 72, 40, 48, 24
2. 27, 81, 56, 18, 32
3. 72, 0, 16, 64, 54
4. 36, 63, 9, 32, 0
5. 27, 40, 63, 8, 45;
Circle: 8 in Row 5, 9 in Row 4, 16 in
Row 3, 18 in Row 2, 24 in Row 1

Page 18

x	0	1	2	3	4	5	6	7	8	9
0	0	0	0	0	0	0	0	0	0	0
1	0	1	2	3	4	5	6	7	8	9
2	0	2	4	6	8	10	12	14	16	18
3	0	3	6	9	12	15	18	21	24	27
4	0	4	8	12	16	20	24	28	32	36
5	0	5	10	15	20	25	30	35	40	45
6	0	6	12	18	24	30	36	42	48	54
7	0	7	14	21	28	35	42	49	56	63
8	0	8	16	24	32	40	48	56	64	72
9	0	9	18	27	36	45	54	63	72	81

1. 3, 2, 9   2. 6, 6, 8
3. 9, 8, 2   4. 7, 9, 6

Page 19

28 tiles

Page 20

Page 21

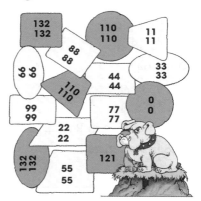

132 132
110 110
11 11
88 88
66 66
33 33
110 110
44 44
0 0
99 99
77 77
22 22
132 132
55 55
121

Page 22

1. 0, 48, 84, 120

2. 12, 60, 96, 132

3. 24, 72, 108, 144

4. 36

```
O N E H U N D R E D T H I R T Y – T W O
R N F X W F R Q R I P D B Q E H B H O P
E Q E Z T O O U C Z G S C I O D M I A F
O N E H U N D R E D E I G H T R T R T O
Y W I L U I G U N N R X D W L E N H Y R
M T E N V N H W T H I R T Y – S I X G T
E W F O N E D U K D L E A T R E B C Y Y
Y N O H S Y H H H E I G H T Y – F O U R
P T I U E G V B D H I D W N Q J N T D
L Y W N X S L I E E T R J E I G H Y D
D D T H V I O W S N Y W J K F L B T N H
A F S I X T Y O E T X E K O L V C K T
K O U G E U Y R E N I Y O N R Y V E T Z
T U R H U V D D Z S E V E N T Y – T W O
F R E S O N E F T E T Y F I X Y A Y E C
A N T F V U R N O R R M S O U T Y I R J
O N E H U N D R E D F O R T Y – F O U R
```

Page 23

1. 12 × 7 = 84, 12 × 0 = 0

2. 12 × 8 = 96, 12 × 11 = 132,
   12 × 6 = 72, 12 × 12 = 144,
   12 × 3 = 36

3. 12 × 1 = 12, 12 × 5 = 60,
   12 × 7 = 84, 12 × 9 = 108,
   12 × 4 = 48

4. 12 × 10 = 120, 12 × 4 = 48,
   12 × 8 = 96, 12 × 11 = 132,
   12 × 2 = 24;

72 sentences; Answers will vary.

Page 24

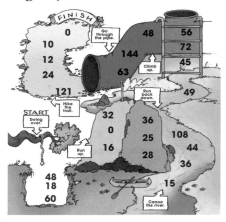

Page 25

A. 100	G. 3	N. 96	S. 54
B. 42	H. 81	O. 36	T. 0
C. 30	I. 72	P. 132	U. 40
E. 49	L. 24	Q. 64	V. 21
F. 27	M. 18	R. 20	Y. 16;

EVERY PROBLEM THEY
ENCOUNTER IN LIFE BECOMES
A CHALLENGE TO CONQUER!

Page 26

24, 32, 30, 42, 45; 32 balls

Page 27

U. 46	A. 36	Q. 28	E. 93
E. 99	J. 213	D. 166	! 88
C. 48	N. 55	A. 129	S. 148
R. 208	S. 66; SQUARE DANCERS!		

Page 28

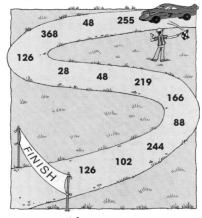

3 × 32 = 96 laps

Page 29

1. 628, 690

2. 1,296, 2,084

3. 1,208, 2,106

4. 2,169, 1,842, 482, 2,439

5. 336, 248, 909, 2,480;

3 × 112 = 336 tubes

Page 30

1. 609, 822, 310, 636

2. 770, 282, 390, 906

3. 228, 524, 999, 460;

Review colored apples.

102 × 4 = 408 apples

Page 31

1. 144, 125, 441

2. 664, 432, 116, 282, 385

3. 310, 192, 290, 147, 384

Page 32

N. 204   C. 51   A. 184   H. 310

I. 318   B. 504   S. 112   K. 96

R. 108   B. 117; IN BRANCH BANKS

Page 33

1. 159, 126, 184, 292

2. 204, 328, 175, 108

3. 150, 161, 156, 64

4. 58, 190, 288, 168;

Circle: 53 × 3, 63 × 2, 82 × 4,

52 × 3, 32 × 2, 84 × 2;

2 problems in row A and C,

1 problem in row B and D

Page 34

1. 72 × 4 = 288¢   2. 29 × 6 = 174¢

3. 68 × 3 = 204¢   4. 87 × 3 = 261¢

5. 43 × 2 = 86¢, 29 × 2 = 58¢,
   86 + 58 = 144¢

6. 95 × 3 = 285¢, 68 × 2 = 136¢,
   285 + 136 = 421¢

Page 35

G. 1,536   T. 938   S. 1,431

I. 4,992   A. 2,739   D. 3,528

M. 1,092   E. 840   N. 1,992

R. 3,450   K. 4,896   H. 5,208;

NIGHTMARES; 1,632 kg

Page 36

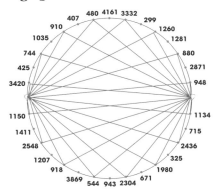

Page 37

1. 2,835   2. 1,824   3. 3,375

4. 5,348   5. 1,752   6. 2,904

7. 1,564   8. 3,192   9. 3,232

10. 2,430

Page 38

Game 1:

392 O	1,032 O	126 X
714 O	1,506 X	528 X
248 X	332 O	370 O

Game 2:

291 O	756 X	896 X
304 O	440 O	756 X
900 O	608 X	174 O

Page 39

1. 90   2. 300   3. 130   4. 370

5. 700   6. 800   7. 900   8. 250

9. 60   10. 500   11. 80   12. 600

Pages 40–41

1. $3 \times 78 = 234$ scoops

2. $8 \times 2 = 16$ shoes

3. $48 \times 6 = 288$ treats

4. $3 \times \$265 = \$795$

5. $3 \times 24 = 72$ 6. $4 \times 5 = 20$

Page 42

1. $10 \div 5 = 2$ 2. $10 \div 2 = 5$

Page 43

Review grouping.

1. 4   2. 2   3. 4   4. 5

5. 6   6. 3   7. 8   8. 5

Page 44

1. 3, 3, 5 2. 4, 7, 4 3. 1, 6, 8

4. 6, 7   5. 2, 1   6. 5, 8; $18 \div 6 = 3$

Page 45

Review drawing.

1. 4, 9, 1, 6   2. 5, 3, 8, 2   3. 8, 4, 5

4. 3, 1, 8, 9   5. 5, 2, 4, 2

Page 46

1. 6, 8, 9, 1   2. 9, 5, 5, 7

3. 2, 4, 8, 9, 5   4. 3, 7, 2, 3, 6

5. 3 kites;   9 kites of each color

Page 47

1. 6, 9, 6   2. 4, 9, 8

3. 2, 8, 4   4. 7, 10, 7

5. 8 students 6. 4 monkeys

Page 48

1. 5, 4, 2, 8 2. 7, 3, 5, 1

3. 3, 1, 7   4. 2, 4, 6

5. 0, 1, 2, 3, 4, 5, 6, 7, 8, 9

6. 0, 1, 2, 3, 4, 5, 6, 7, 8, 9;

Circle: $30 \div 6 = 5$.

Page 49

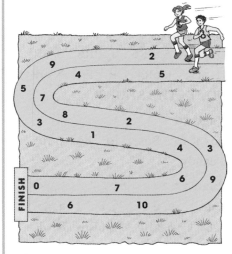

9 km

Page 50

Circle: 1, 3, 5, 6, 7, 10, 11, 12, 14;

2 km

Page 51

1. 22, 24, 31, 13

2. 32, 21, 34, 10

3. 33, 23, 40, 11

Page 52

1. 29, 17, 12, 18   2. 16, 12, 37, 23

3. 13, 19, 13, 15;   29 marbles

Page 53

1. 1R4, 4R1

2. 6R2, 9R1, 7R5, 6R5

3. 7R2, 7R1, 7R1, 6R6

4. 5R1, 6R2, 3R1, 5R2;

6 hurdles

Page 54

1. 8R1, 8R4, 6R1, 9R2

2. 7R1, 6R1, 5R3, 5R1

3. 4R1, 5R1, 8R2, 7R1

4. 3R2, 3R1, 9R2, 5R6

5. 4R1, 6R3, 2R4, 6R2;

7 apples

Page 55

I. 9R3 L. 9R2 S. 9R4 O. 4R4

T. 3R5 N. 7R5 P. 6R4 I. 7R3

O. 4R3 A. 8R6 T. 8R2 S. 6R1

H. 5R3 !. 6R3 R. 5R2 N. 9R7;

NO, ON THE STAIRS!

Page 56

Box 1: 10 Box 2: 10 Box 3: 10;

2 candy

Page 57

1. 4 2. 2 3. 6 4. 5

5. 8 6. 3R2 7. 6R6 8. 9R2

9. 8R1 10. 15R2;

"MULTI" PILERS

Page 58

1. 63, 24, 36, 35 2. 9, 18, 48, 81

3. 32, 21, 16, 18 4. 64, 9, 30, 7

5. 160, 90, 300 6. 420, 300, 80;

128 people

Pages 59–60

1. 4 sweaters with 2 left over

2. 6 candy canes 3. 7 cookies

4. 2 cars 5. 2 cans 6. 9

Page 61

1. 96 ÷ 6 = 16 cookies

2. 98 ÷ 9 = 10R8, 10 candy bars,
   8¢ left over

3. 72 ÷ 4 = 18 bags of jelly beans

4. 84 ÷ 6 = 14 cookies

5. 63 ÷ 5 = 12R3, 12 candy canes

6. 74 ÷ 7 = 10R4, 10 pieces of
   licorice and 1 bag of jelly beans

Page 62

1. 2 × 3 = 6, 3 × 2 = 6,
   6 ÷ 2 = 3, 6 ÷ 3 = 2

2. 2 × 8 = 16, 8 × 2 = 16,
   16 ÷ 2 = 8, 16 ÷ 8 = 2

3. 4 × 5 = 20, 5 × 4 = 20,
   20 ÷ 4 = 5, 20 ÷ 5 = 4

4. 3 × 5 = 15, 5 × 3 = 15,
   15 ÷ 3 = 5, 15 ÷ 5 = 3

5. 3 × 9 = 27, 9 × 3 = 27,
   27 ÷ 3 = 9, 27 ÷ 9 = 3

6. 3 × 12 = 36, 12 × 3 = 36,
   36 ÷ 3 = 12, 36 ÷ 12 = 3

7. 5 × 6 = 30, 6 × 5 = 30,
   30 ÷ 5 = 6, 30 ÷ 6 = 5

8. 6 × 7 = 42, 7 × 6 = 42,
   42 ÷ 6 = 7, 42 ÷ 7 = 6

9. 4 × 8 = 32, 8 × 4 = 32,
   32 ÷ 4 = 8, 32 ÷ 8 = 4;
   33 ÷ 3 = 11 marbles;
   3, 11, 33

Page 63

1. 3 × 4 = 12, 4 × 3 = 12,
   12 ÷ 3 = 4, 12 ÷ 4 = 3

2. 5 × 7 = 35, 7 × 5 = 35,
   35 ÷ 5 = 7, 35 ÷ 7 = 5

3. 3 × 7 = 21, 7 × 3 = 21,
   21 ÷ 3 = 7, 21 ÷ 7 = 3

4. 6 × 4 = 24, 4 × 6 = 24,
   24 ÷ 6 = 4, 24 ÷ 4 = 6

5. 7 × 8 = 56, 8 × 7 = 56,
   56 ÷ 7 = 8, 56 ÷ 8 = 7

6. 3 × 6 = 18, 6 × 3 = 18,
   18 ÷ 3 = 6, 18 ÷ 6 = 3

Page 64

1. 560, 3,000, 27,000, 440,
   240, 12,000

2. 490, 36,000, 5,400, 42,000,
   3,500, 360

3. 48,000, 480, 240, 4,500,
   24,000, 400

Page 65

1. 70, 900, 90, 900, 800

2. 600, 80, 900, 80, 80

3. 50, 90, 800, 60, 80

Page 66

1. 2 × 6 = 12 2. 8 × 4 = 32

3. 9 × 3 = 27 4. 7 × 3 = 21

5. 9 × 5 = 45 6. 7 × 6 = 42

7. 4 × 7 = 28 8. 12 × 3 = 36

9. 8 × 9 = 72 10. 5 × 6 = 30

11. 10 × 4 = 40 12. 7 × 9 = 63

13. 11 × 2 = 22 14. 11 × 12 = 132

Page 67

1. 36 2. 155 3. 248 4. 86

5. 104 6. 216 7. 6 8. 7

9. 6 10. 8 11. 12 12. 16

Pages 68–69

1. Ellen 2. 162 3. 20

4. 48 5. 9 6. 400¢

Pages 70–74

1. A 2. A 3. A 4. B

5. C 6. C 7. D 8. C

9. B 10. C 11. A

12. $47 × 22 = $1,034

13. 200 × 5 = 1,000

14. 80 × 4 = 320

15. 50 ÷ 5 = 10

16. 81 ÷ 9 = 9

17. 72 ÷ 6 = 12

SCHOLASTIC

Learning Express

Congratulations!

I, _____

am a Scholastic Superstar!

Paste a photo or draw a picture of yourself.

I have completed Multiplication and Division L3.

Presented on _____